Learning from Religi

The Muslim Way

April Heywood

Hodder & Stoughton

ACKNOWLEDGEMENTS

I am very grateful to Kevin O'Donnell for giving me the opportunity to write this book. Without his encouragement, I would not have felt brave enough at all to attempt it. I must also thank Dr Z H Zaidi for affirming the direction in which I felt impelled to go. My interviews with him, Dr A A Mughram of the Regent's Park Mosque, and Mr Abdul Dayan Khizri, Imam of the Aylesbury Mosque, stimulated so many ideas for the book. I must also thank Mr Muhammad Usamah, Education Officer of the Muslim Educational Trust for his correspondence and constructive help.

Finally, without the support and active sacrifices of my family – my husband, Colin and my children, Matthew, Elizabeth and Caroline – this book would not have been written.

The publishers would like to thank the following for permission to reproduce copyright material in this volume:

The Independent for extracts from the article 'Dear Mike Tyson' by Abdal Hakim Murad.

The publishers would also like to thank the following for permission to reproduce copyright illustrations in this volume:

Andes Press Agency/Carlos Reyes p6, 10, 42; Greg Evans International/Greg Balfour Evans p46; Colin Heywood p43, 44; The Kobal Collection © Walt Disney Pictures p6; *The Independent*/Herbie Knott p 40; Popperfoto p22 (Rula Halawani), 47 (right); Rex Features – Sipa Press p36, 47 (left); Peter Sanders p11, 13; Science Photo Library/Petit Format/Nestle p26; Trip p5 (H Rogers), 6 (H Rogers top right), 7, 8 (H Rogers top right), 10, 11, 12, 21, 22 (Mark Rogers), 26 (G Howe top right, V Shuba bottom right), 28, 35, 48.

Every effort has been made to trace and acknowledge ownership of copyright. The publishers will be glad to make suitable arrangements with any copyright holders whom it has not been possible to contact.

Illustrated by Joseph McEwan

British Library Cataloguing in Publication Data

Heywood, April
   The Muslim way. – (Learning from religion)
   1. Islam – Juvenile literature
   I. Title
   297

ISBN 0 340 639 202

First published 1997
Impression number   10 9 8 7 6 5 4 3 2 1
Year   1999   1998   1997

Typeset by Fakenham Photosetting Limited, Fakenham, Norfolk.
Printed in Great Britain for Hodder & Stoughton Educational, a division of Hodder Headline Plc, 338 Euston Road, London, NW1 3BH by Cambus Litho, East Kilbride.

CONTENTS

For the Teacher   4
Student Introduction   5

1   The Muslim Way   8
    A Childhood Memory   8
    A World Religion   9
    Ummah – Community   10
    The Messenger   12

2   Names – Who Am I?   14
    Islam – A Special Relationship   15
    In The Name Of God   17

3   Beliefs   18
    The Five Pillars of Islam   18
    Why Are You Doing That?   19
    Who Do You Say Jesus Was?   20
    The One God   21
    Jihad   22
    Life After Death   24

4   Care of the Earth   25
    Creation   25
    The Environment   26
    Animal Rights   27

5   The Word   28
    Waiting for the Word   28
    Read!   29
    People of the Book   30
    The Word Revealed   32

6   Journeys   33
    Hajj   34
    A Journey Of Self-Discovery – The Hajj   35
    The Mosque   37
    Prayer – Coming Closer To God   38
    Prayer – How We Do It   39

7   Community   40
    A Western Religion   40
    Sharing – Zakat   41
    Muslims Together – Ramadan   42
    Saving Up for the Cause of God   43

8   Differences   45
    Teenagers   45
    How Do We Get On With People?   46
    From Confrontation Towards a New
      Understanding   47

FOR THE TEACHER

I do not think that it is possible for anyone to appreciate what it is like to be a Muslim, unless one is a Muslim. I do not think that it is possible for a Muslim to appreciate and understand all that there is to be known about Islam, any more than it is for a Christian to know all that there is about Christianity. However, I think that it is possible for a non-believer to learn something about Islam, to appreciate its impact on different civilisations of the world, and to understand some aspects of what it is like to live as a Muslim in Britain today.

I also think that it is possible to relate something of one's personal experience to that of other people, no matter how young or old, and then to learn from that spiritual exchange. It is on that basis that I have written this book.

The experiential approach to Religious Education begins with day-to-day familiarity. In Chapter 2, *Names*, there is a new pupil at school. Other pupils introduce themselves. They want to 'suss' him out. One of the others is a Muslim. The new boy has never heard a traditional Muslim name before and his curiosity is aroused. He wants to know more. The Muslim boy has red hair: his parents are converts to Islam and they have adopted an orthodox Muslim lifestyle. Just as the boy's parents were obliged to confront basic issues, including the acquisition of some understanding of the sacred language of Islam, classical Arabic, so we, too have to confront similar problems.

I have attempted to devise supporting activities and worksheets in such a way which will allow pupils to use their imagination as the stimulus to understanding. Traditional Muslim names, for instance, are the most immediate feature about a Muslim which informs the rest of us of his or her religion. There is a simple 'game' which utilises classical Arabic naming structures, giving a glimpse of how Muslims name their children and how important the family is in Islam.

Pupils are asked to use their imaginations to understand how the Prophet Muhammad received his first revelations, in Chapter 1. He was a man chosen by God, and in the Sirah he is described as reacting in fear and disbelief to the manifestation of the Archangel Gabriel and what he was asked to do. Pupils are asked to write an account, with supporting pictures, putting themselves in a position like Muhammad's. Firstly, it is hoped they will get a flavour of the story itself. Secondly, they will be expected to use their own creative talents around the story. Thirdly, they will have developed a response to a basic Muslim theological belief that Muhammad was a mere mortal who was selected to carry the burden of revealing God's word, which is called the Qur'an. The Qur'an itself is revelation in Muslim doctrine, just as the person of Jesus is for Christians.

STUDENT INTRODUCTION

Most of you will know something about Islam, some of you more than others. The word Islam can be used to describe the religious beliefs of millions of Muslims worldwide. Islam, or Islamic, is sometimes used to describe a way of life or culture which has developed over the centuries.

Here are some pictures taken from different parts of the world. All of these have something to do with Islam.

Wandering tribes still live in the deserts of Arabia and surrounding countries just as they did 1,400 years ago when Muhammad, the founder of Islam, was alive. But now they have to live among the oil wells which have had a great influence on the economies of some Arab countries. This has made the oil wells a target during wartime. The second picture shows Kuwaiti oil wells blown up during the Gulf War of 1990–91.

An oil lake, Burgan Oil Fields, Kuwait.

THE WORLD OF ISLAM

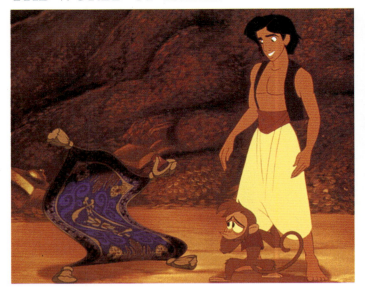

This picture shows Muslim children. Some Muslims dress in a special way to show that they are Muslim, but not all.

The story of 'Aladdin' comes from *The Tales of A Thousand and One Nights*. The mosque pictured below is in Britain. Both come from the Islamic tradition but the film is American and the mosque was designed by a non-Muslim architect.

All Muslims accept an obligation to go on pilgrimage to the sacred mosque in Makkah, the birthplace of their founder. It is here that they perform the special ceremonies connected with the Ka'aba, shown above.

THINGS TO DO

1 In groups, think about more examples of Islam or Islamic culture.

2 You may not yet know very much about Islam, but what do you think it is about the pictures shown here, which might give them a connection with Islam?

A FEW THINGS YOU NEED TO KNOW

Islam originated in Arabia but today it is an international religion. Although followers of Islam speak many different languages, when it comes to the practice of their religion and declaring their faith, they continue to use the language itself of the first Muslims. That language is Arabic.

In English, religious people call the Creator of all things God. So do I, because I am English. But because I am also a Muslim, I sometimes use the Arabic name, which is Allah

The religion which Allah created for mankind is Islam

Someone who believes in Islam is called a Muslim

The name of the Prophet to whom God revealed His Will is Muhammad. To show respect we often repeat afer mentioning him: 'Praises and blessings be upon him'

When written down, this is often shortened to the letters, **pbuh**. Whenever Muslims mention the name of anyone else who is particularly special to Islam, they will also acknowledge their importance by saying these words or others like them; for instance, after the names of other prophets, such as **Abraham (Ibrahim** in Arabic) and **Moses (Musa)**, **Jesus (Isa)**.

THINGS TO DO

1 In groups, think about how you would make up your mind about someone you were about to meet, but had not yet spoken to. For instance, what clues would they give – about their personality, their interests, and their nationality and possibly their religion – in the way they stand or walk, or in how they dress? Think about yourself in this way too.

God's word was revealed to Muhammad in stages and, after a while, was collected together and written down in a book. This book is known as **The Holy Qur'an**, *the Holy Sayings of God.*

1

THE MUSLIM WAY

A Childhood Memory . . . The Call to Prayer

Imagine a child lying in bed. The sun is rising in the morning sky. The child, a girl, is beginning to stir. The day begins early in Malaya because by lunchtime it is too hot to do much. School starts at 8 o'clock and children like this girl are accustomed to rising early, getting into the shower and dressed, having breakfast, and schoolbag packed in readiness to catch the school bus by 7.30.

But today, it is not quite 6 o'clock. She snuggles back under the sheet to snatch a few more moments in bed.

Then she hears the call to prayer from the nearby mosque. Almost in unison, the call issues from mosques further away. The rhythms of the familiar but ancient summons to believers rise and fall. A song both strange and reassuring sounds in her head. She does not understand the words but she feels the rhythm, the intonation. Now long, a plea to all who hear to attend the Lord. Now short, abrupt even. *You must come **now**.*

A chorus of **syncopation** (not quite together), the rhythm repeats until the message has been sent out and the last voice rests. It is now just after 6 o'clock. Time to rise and begin the day. That child was me.

I am not a Muslim but the magic of the Muslim call to prayer, the **adhan**, has remained with me. It kindled in me a profound interest and regard for Islam. Even today, the adhan arouses in me an emotional response.

I come from an Anglican background. The adhan belongs to that part of me which I describe as my spiritual self.

The Call to Prayer was and is universal. It calls to everyone. Whether a person listens to it is up to the individual. The intention is to remind people of an existence outside and greater than their own lives. This much I sensed rather than understood as a child.

THINGS TO DO

1 What do you think is meant by:
   (a) 'the familiar but ancient summons'
   (b) 'a chorus of syncopation'?

2 Have you got any memories which stir a strong but good feeling inside you? What is the best way of explaining this to others? As a class, discuss the different ways in which you could adequately express your feelings, e.g. as a story, a poem, a painting, or on the sports field.

3 Some people's most powerful memories can be painful and disturbing. Is it possible for memories like these to be told to others? How might you try to tell these to other people?

A World Religion

Country (Majority of population)	Population in millions		
Indonesia	200	Saudi Arabia	17
Pakistan	121	Syria	14
Bangladesh	111	Yemen	13
Nigeria	89	Somalia	10
Turkey	62	Azerbaijan	7
Iran	61	Tajikistan	6
Egypt	59	Kyrgyzstan	5
Morocco	29		
Algeria	26	(Minority populations)	Millions
Sudan	26	India	132
Uzbekistan	22	China	107
Iraq	20	Russia	25
Malaysia	19	Philippines	7
Afghanistan	18	USA	6
Kazakhstan	17	Myanmar (Burma)	5
		Bosnia-Herzogovina	4
		United Kingdom	2

According to a recent assessment, the world population of Muslims is over 1,300 million.

THINGS TO DO

1 Every year, at the time of Hajj, millions of Muslims travel to Makkah to participate in the ceremonies. They come from all over the globe bringing their different backgrounds and cultures, as well as the faith they share with everyone. Write a poem or draw a picture which expresses such a variety of experience.

2 An activity to be done individually or in groups.
a) Imagine that you work for a large charity with contacts abroad. What has the charity been set up to do?
b) Decide on a name and a logo for your charity.
c) How do you feel about the work of your charity? Write two paragraphs explaining your commitment to its work.

Ummah . . . Community

Thus have We made of you
An Ummah justly balanced,
That ye might be witnesses
Over the nations,
And an Apostle a witness
Over yourselves
(*Sura* ii:143)

This quotation from the Qur'an shows how important it is for Muslims to have a sense of community and togetherness. The Arabic word for this is **Ummah**.

The Muslim community is not just a group of people following a particular religion. Muslims have a responsibility to all people to show that they have accepted that they have to live in a world consisting of different beliefs and attitudes and customs.

Muslims are identified by their *Apostle*, who is their Prophet Muhammad. Under his guidance, Muslims will behave responsibly and with justice in the world. They have also a responsibility towards each other.

In Britain, Muslims have had to adjust to living in a multiracial society. Muslim men and women work with people from other cultures.

Muslim children attend school where there may very well be an overall domination of one religion, e.g. Christianity.

Muslim people also show an awareness of religious identity when they come together as part of religious observance.

For instance, at prayer:

on pilgrimage:

when a baby is born:

when people get married:

and when someone dies.

These examples are taken from special occasions. At other times Muslims sometimes show their consciousness of belonging to the Islamic community by wearing a particular style of clothing.

THINGS TO DO

1 The Muslim community has a well developed sense of belonging. You have been invited to a birthday party for your Muslim friend. Many of his/her relatives are already there when you arrive. You are introduced to several of his/her friends, who do not go to your school, but attend the local mosque. They are all very welcoming, and you soon relax and feel at home. Write two to three paragraphs about attending your friend's party.

2 In groups of three or four, make a presentation on A3 paper, in words and pictures, of what you understand by the Arabic word, *ummah*.

3 Individually, or in groups, or as a class make a picture, mural or a collage, which shows something of what it means to be a Muslim in the world community. You need to think of images from both inside and outside Islamic culture.

The Messenger . . .

Makkah, the birthplace of Muhammad, as it looks today.

In Muslim tradition, there have been many messengers seeking to guide mankind towards the True Religion (**Din**, pronounced 'Deen') of God (**Allah**). These were the prophets of the Jews and Christians, like Adam, Abraham (**Ibrahim**), Moses (**Musa**), and Jesus (**Isa**). Yet somehow humankind was still going wrong.

Then in a desert land, many miles from the centres of the known world of the seventh century CE, the last of the Prophets appeared from among the tribes of Arabia. His name was **Muhammad**.

Muhammad's message to his fellow tribesmen was clear:

> 'Reject all idols. They are false Gods. Worship the One True God (**Allah**). Submission (**Islam**) to his will means that your place in Paradise is assured.'

Not all his fellow tribesmen of the tribe of **Quraysh** in the town of **Makkah** accepted **Muhammad's** message. Those who did were persecuted by the many who did not. The early believers in **Islam**, who were called **Muslims**, suffered many abuses, some were murdered. Eventually Muhammad decided to move to anywhere which would accept him and his followers.

To the north of Makkah was a town called **Yathrib**. The people of this town were looking for a wise leader to rule them because there had been many disputes among the five tribes who lived there.

Representatives of the town had heard of the new Prophet living in Makkah, and asked Muhammad to come to Yathrib to be their leader.

Muhammad agreed. It was the ideal solution. In 622 CE he and his followers moved to Yathrib which was renamed the City of the Prophet, **Madinat al-Nabi**. It is now simply referred to as **Madina**.

MARCH

Ramadan/Shawwal 1413 AH					
Saturday		6 13	13 20	20 27	27 4
Sunday		7 14	14 21	21 28	28 5
Monday	1 8	8 15	15 22	22 29	29 6
Tuesday	2 9	9 16	16 23	23 30	30 7
Wednesday	3 10	10 17	17 24	24 1	31 8
Thursday	4 11	11 18	18 25	25 2	
Friday	5 12	12 19	19 26	26 3	

The Muslim calendar takes its name and dates from the migration to Madina, **al Hijra** (AH). Year one of the Muslim calendar is 622 of the Common Era (CE). All Muslim countries use the Muslim calendar. There is a mathematical formula to convert calendar years from one era to the other. Muslims living in Britain have a calendar which shows both eras so they know when Muslim festivals are to take place.

. . . Muhammad

The Prophet's Mosque in Madina. The green dome was built above Muhammad's tomb.

Hostilities broke out between Makkah and Madina, which were finally resolved when Muhammad conquered Makkah in AH 8/630 CE. Muhammad immediately set about restoring the rituals and practices of the Din of Allah. The House of Allah, the **Ka'aba**, was cleansed of its many figures of gods and goddesses and returned to its central place as the focus for the worship of Allah. The annual pilgrimage (the **Hajj**) was purified by removing its pagan rituals.

In Muslim tradition Adam was not only the first human but the first of the Prophets. Muhammad became known as the **Seal of the Prophets** or the last prophet. There are many traditions about Muhammad but a biography (known as the **Sirah**) was written about a hundred years after his death by **Muhammad ibn Ishaq**, and has become the accepted standard account of Muhammad's life. Ibn Ishaq's version was the only one to survive intact in a copy written by one of his pupils, **Ibn Hisham**.

Muhammad is not worshipped for he was a man. Worship is reserved for Allah alone. Muhammad is special because he was chosen by Allah as His Messenger to reveal His words or sayings (Qur'an) to all people.

Muslims everywhere acknowledge how special Muhammad is by saying 'Praises and blessings be upon him' whenever they speak his name. (This is frequently shortened in textbooks to 'pbuh'.)

Chronology
570 CE Birth of Muhammad in Makkah
610 CE Called to Prophethood
622 CE The Hijra to Madina
630 CE Conquest of Makkah
632 CE Death of Muhammad

THINGS TO DO

1 Why do you think that the Muslim calendar begins with the Hijra and not before?

2 On one sheet of paper, write your own biography. What would you put in and what would you leave out?

3 Why do you think that it was 100 years before a standard biography of Muhammad to be written?

4 'Muhammad is the Messenger of God.' What do you think a Muslim means by that?

NAMES – WHO AM I?

Have you ever thought about what your name means? Most of us have some idea of what our name means or where it comes from. For example, the name Clare (or the alternative, Claire) comes from the French 'clair' which means 'bright' or 'clear'. It refers to how something can be pale, bright and pure, all at the same time, like the light of the full moon. You may be familiar with the phrase 'au clair de la lune' which means 'by moonlight'.

The name Peter means 'a rock' and, in Christianity, was the name given to Jesus' first disciple.

Murad comes from an Arabic word, meaning 'the one who was most wanted'. Most Muslim names are Arabic-based because Arabic was the language of the first Muslims. To be a Muslim is to belong to a living tradition which harks back to over 1,400 years. Muslims of today come from different countries all over the world and speak many different languages. However, through their names, Muslims feel that they share their rich heritage with the earliest Muslims.

Murad was the name of an important Sultan (a ruler) of the Ottoman Empire. The Ottoman Empire was founded in about 1299 CE, and was ruled from Istanbul, in present day Turkey. It reached its peak in the fifteenth and sixteenth centuries. The Ottoman Empire fell into a long decline, which ended only in 1918 after the First World War.

Hi, my name is Murad. What's yours?

Mor-what?

H-hi. It's Peter. Sorry, but could you say your name again? I don't think I heard it right the first time

It's pronounced M-U-R-A-D

THINGS TO DO

1 Try to find out what your name means. In small groups, discuss what your name means, or what or who it refers to. Then share with the rest of the class.

2 Draw a picture of yourself, using the letters of your name as part of the design.

3 Write a short story or play about one or two of your friends (these could be imaginary) and say whether or not their names suit them.

Islam . . . A Special Relationship

Murad and the new boy, Peter, are beginning to forge a new friendship, a relationship. They are curious about each other and ask questions about:

Their families

Their interests and hobbies

Who they admire

Peter has never before met someone who calls himself a Muslim and wants to know more about what that means. He asks Murad why he is a Muslim.

Murad explains:

'There are lots of ways to explain what it means to be a Muslim. But I think that the most important is to say that I believe in God and that the word Muslim describes a kind of relationship with God. I was born a Muslim, but my parents weren't. They both decided to become Muslim before I was born, (they **converted** to Islam) and had to learn to read the Qur'an, the Holy Book of Islam. They had to learn Arabic, the language in which the Holy Qur'an is written. None of my grandparents is Muslim. My Mum's family comes from Cornwall, and my Dad's from London, and we visit them as often as we can. Both my parents go out to work and so, if we have not seen my grandparents for a while, they come and visit us.'

THINGS TO DO

1 Draw a family tree, explaining the relationship of members of your family with yourself. You do not need to go further back than grandparents, unless you want to in the time available.

2 In small groups decide what the word 'convert' means. Then think of situations where someone is a convert. Present your idea(s) to the rest of the class.

3 Murad's beliefs are special to him. Write a poem or a story about a special friend or relation or pet. Say what is special about them and why.

The Blue Mosque, Istanbul, Turkey.

You are alone under the dome. You are small in this vastness. But you are not afraid because you also know that you are meant to feel that this is your natural place. The prayer hall has been designed for people to come together, or just on their own, to concentrate on the worship of God.

The design reflects the relationship of humanity to God, which is called **Islam**. Islam is usually defined as the complete surrender, or submission, of people to God. This is taken to mean that a person must give the whole of him or herself to God and His laws. But the Arabic root of the word Islam (**s-l-m**) has a basic idea of safety and security. This means that a Muslim – a person who takes on Islam – becomes a whole person, because to surrender completely to the will of God is to lose oneself in the feeling of safety and well-being which comes with faith.

The picture above shows the interior of a mosque built over 300 years ago. Imagine how big the mosque must be, inside and out. The walls inside are covered in the most beautiful and intricate tiles and mosaics. The main colours of blue, white and gold are worked into complex abstract patterns and inscriptions taken from the Holy Book of Islam, the Qur'an. The design is planned so that the eye of the onlooker is not drawn to any fixed point and is free to look around, anywhere. Just as God is anywhere and everywhere.

Standing underneath this huge and beautiful dome, you are meant to feel that you are small and insignificant. Everything around you is huge and vast and reminds you of the hugeness and vastness of God. Yet you know that even this wonderful and spectacular building is as nothing compared to God.

THINGS TO DO

1 Imagine that you are inside the Masjid-i Shah. Write a paragraph describing some of the decoration and comment on how this and the size of the building affect you.

2 Write a short play about two friends. (A) has invited (B) to tea at his/her house for the first time. B is very shy and nervous about meeting A's family and A has to convince B that everything will be all right. When they arrive at A's house, B is made to feel very welcome by A's parents and soon relaxes and begins to feel at home.

3 Design the interior of a magnificent building (you can choose any type of building) and say, in a paragraph underneath, what people are meant to feel inside it. Think also about what the purpose of the building is.

In the Name of God . . . 99 Names of God

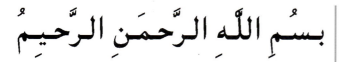

This is a written statement in Arabic, which declares;

'In the name of God, the Most Gracious and the Most Merciful.' (The opening words of The Qur'an.)

The words in italics (referred to as the **Bismillah** in Arabic) always precede any sacred writing in Islam, and, because Muslims believe that God is involved in all human activity, the Bismillah is very often said or written at the beginning of other important or everyday events.

Unlike some other world religions, no visual images of God exist in Islam. Muslims believe it is impossible to think of what God could possibly look like in ordinary human terms. God **is**, and **has existed** and **will exist** for all time.

Instead, Muslims have over the centuries made pictures out of the words of God and have made statements about God. The art of Arabic calligraphy has been developed to heights of exquisite beauty. The words themselves and the writings about God, help Muslims to think about God.

God! there is no god
But He! To Him belong
The Most Beautiful Names.
(Qur'an 20:8, p791)

The usual name for God in Islam is the Arabic word, **Allah, the One God**. Because God is all powerful, it is therefore fitting that He should be given the most beautiful names. The tradition has developed since the days of early Islam that there are 99 names for God. Muslims will think, or meditate, on the Names of God as part of worship to help them approach nearer to the mystery of God. Although, as believers will tell you, mere humans cannot possibly hope to understand the smallest part of God. God is above all human understanding.

The Names describe a characteristic or attribute of God. A few of these are:

The Merciful	**The King**
The Peace	**The Hearer**
The Revealer	**The Truth**
The Allpowerful	**The Light**
The Holy One	**The High One**
The Eternal	**The First and the Last**

THINGS TO DO

1 Using your imagination, make a shape or abstract design from the letters of the name of your school and, if you wish, include the school motto.

2 Write a short sentence explaining what you think each of the Names of God mentioned above means. Then write a short paragraph about three of them, linking them with an example taken from everyday life or from your imagination.

3 Write a song, a poem, or a prayer about one of the Names of God.

3

BELIEFS

Five Pillars of Islam

There are five main beliefs in Islam, and because everything else in Islam is connected with them in one way or another, they are sometimes referred to as The Five Pillars of Islam.

The most important belief is:

> There is only one God and Muhammad is his prophet

This declaration is called the **shahadah**.

The others are:

> We must pray to God five times a day

> We must not eat during the day in the month of Ramadan

Prayer is called **salah**. This fasting is called **sawm**.

> We have to give money to the poor and needy

> There is a box for this in the mosque. But there are charities which we support too

Giving money and other means of support is called **zakat**.

> We must go on a pilgrimage to the Ka'aba, in Makkah, at least once in our lives. It is called the Hajj

> But it is important that only people go who can afford it, and that they make sure that their family or relatives who are left behind will be all right

> There are special ceremonies which we take part in and which our beloved prophet Muhammad (pbuh), took part in a long time ago

> We believe that people who cannot make the Hajj are taken there spiritually in the love and friendship of those who can

THINGS TO DO

1 List the 5 main beliefs of Islam and give an explanation of each.

2 Why do you think the 5 main beliefs in Islam are called The Five Pillars of Islam? Could they be called anything else? Write a paragraph about this and make a drawing to support your idea.

3 Design your own creed (declaration of beliefs), on your own, in groups, and/or as a class. Try to put all you want to say into 5 main statements.

Why are you doing that?

It is lunchtime at Borrowdale Comprehensive School. The sun is shining and so most of the pupils are eating their lunches outdoors. Peter and Murad are sitting on the grass near the fish pond. Peter has just opened his lunch box.

PETER Great! Mum's put in some sausage rolls. Would you like one?
MURAD (greatly embarrassed) N-No thank you.
PETER Don't you like them? They're very nice.
MURAD No, it's not so much that. I'm not allowed to eat pork. I hope you're not offended.
PETER (amazed) Of course not! But why aren't you?
MURAD Well, it's part of being Muslim. We do things in our everyday lives which show that we are Muslim. It's another way of worshipping God.
PETER But I thought worship was all about praying and . . . well, singing. People don't worship God with their lunches do they?
MURAD Well we do. It says in the Qur'an that we must not eat pork or any meat which has not been prepared in the proper way with the name of God said over it. We don't drink alcohol and Muslim parents are very strict about smoking.
PETER Don't you have any fun at all?
MURAD (laughing) Of course we do. We have parties with music and dancing just like anybody. There are even pop groups with Muslims in them these days. It's just that God is part of our everyday lives and not just to be remembered in the mosque.
PETER Actually, my parents are strict about smoking. It can make you very ill and some people die from it. And it is a good thing to have laws which stop people from drinking too much alcohol, especially if they're driving.

MURAD Of course it is. We respect other people's way of life. Alcohol and smoking are part of the culture here, but I *want* to show that I'm a Muslim by not drinking alcohol, not smoking and not eating pork.
PETER Yes, I think I'm beginning to understand. But do you mind if I finish my sausage rolls?
Murad, grinning, shakes his head.

In Islam the word used to describe things Muslims are not allowed to eat or drink or do, is **haram**. What is allowed is **halal**.

Apart from the laws about food, Muslims are not allowed to involve themselves in anything which leads them to excess. This can be anything intoxicating, like alcohol or drugs (but not as medicine), or gambling.

Going to the cinema is halal, but to view anything excessively violent or pornographic is haram. Excess in anything is unacceptable, even greedy eating habits.

> O ye who believe!
> Make not unlawful
> The good things which God
> Hath made lawful for you,
> But commit no excess:
> For God loveth not
> Those given to excess.
> (*Qur'an* 5:90–93)

THINGS TO DO

1 Remembering that doing anything to excess is unacceptable, or haram, in Islam, list three situations, which you think are haram, and say why.

2 Write a short play between a Muslim and a non-Muslim about what is halal. You can mention food, and/or an alternative situation which describes the opposite of haram.

3 Draw a picture of a room with a table laid with a meal on it. Include items and/or situation(s) which are both halal and haram, and explain why.

Who do you say Jesus was?

MURAD In Islam, Jesus is called **Isa ibn Mariam**, Jesus the son of Mary, and is one of the most important of our prophets.

PETER (surprised) Explain.

MURAD Well, we believe that Jesus foretold that there would be one more prophet after him, and that this was Muhammad. We call Muhammad the 'seal of the prophets' which, we think, means the last of all the prophets.

MURAD Jesus is special to Muslims. He was created by God in a special way, like Adam, who was the first human being to be created. But like all prophets, Jesus was human. Jesus was sent to save mankind by telling people about the One True God and so he is sometimes called **al Masih**, the Messiah or Saviour.

PETER But how is that possible? How can Jesus be both a saviour *and* human?

MURAD As you know, Muslims believe that there is only One God, Who has existed and will exist for all time. God chose to make Jesus in a special way. He was created in Mary by God as a perfect human being. Mary is important, too, as the Virgin Mother of Jesus. But Jesus is only the son of God in the same way as we all are sons and daughters of God.

PETER What other beliefs do you have about Jesus?

MURAD Well, we do not believe in the Trinity, because God is One and cannot be divided. We describe our belief in the One God as **tawhid**, which means literally, the Indivisible One. Because of this, we find it difficult to understand what Christians mean when they talk about the Three in One.

MURAD But we *do* believe that Jesus was a perfect human being, who did no wrong. Because of this, he did not die on a cross, nor was resurrected, but was taken up to Heaven to be with God.

PETER And so, Muslims believe in the Ascension?

MURAD Yes.

THINGS TO DO

1 What do Muslims think of Jesus? List in sentences the beliefs Murad described to Peter.

2 Muslims believe that Muhammad (pbuh) is the 'Seal of the Prophets'. What do you think that means? Write a paragraph, or a poem, describing your ideas.

3 Muslim and Christian beliefs about Jesus have many similarities as well as differences. Divide a page into two columns and list the similarities and differences.

The One God

Say: He is God,
The One and Only;

God, the Eternal, Absolute;

He begetteth not,
Nor is He begotten;

And there is none
Like unto Him.
(Sura 112:1–4)

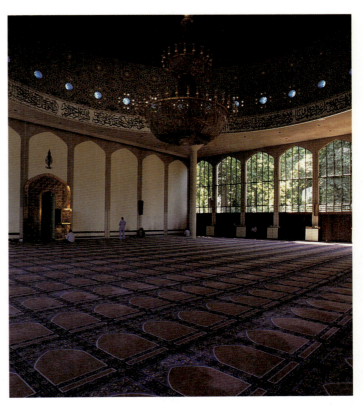

This sura quoted from the Holy Qur'an gives the fundamental doctrine of Islam. There is one God, Who is and always has been. Nothing else created Him and He has not produced any offspring. God is unique and there is no other being which competes with Him. In Arabic this doctrine is called **tawhid**.

No images of any sort are permitted in the mosque because people might worship them instead of God.

God does not exist for humankind; humankind exists for God. People show their relationship with God through the correct observance of prayer and ritual. They perform these rituals not to please themselves but to please God.

God is all powerful, is present everywhere, but is also merciful. He knows that human beings are weak and therefore forgives those who are genuinely sorry for doing wrong.

It is difficult for us to imagine something that goes on forever. One way that human beings can manage is an image of outer space such as the one above.

The uniqueness of God is recognised in the **shahadah**, the Declaration of Faith. In Arabic it sounds like: 'La illa ila lillahu wa Muhammadu rasuluhu,' and can be translated as: 'There is no god but God and Muhammad is His Prophet.'

The mortality of Muhammad is reaffirmed by recognising that he was God's prophet and nothing else.

THINGS TO DO

1 How would you describe eternity? Use pictures and/or words to try this in groups or individually.

2 Regardless of your own beliefs, how do you explain what God is without pictures of Him?

3 The tawhid expresses the 'fundamental doctrine of Islam'. What do you think that means?

Jihad

Muslim women praying at the Dome of the Rock, Jerusalem. A holy city for three religions, Jerusalem has been at the centre of many disputes. When Islam spread, both Jews and Christians were allowed to continue their religions.

According to Muslim tradition, Muslims have an obligation to spread the word of God to those who do not believe in the One True God. During the early period of Islam, this was interpreted as spreading the Word of God through conquest, **jihad**. Following the conquests of the Middle East in the seventh and eighth centuries CE, a sophisticated culture based on Islam developed in these areas.

Other believers in the One True God, the Jews and Christians, were tolerated or given, **dhimmi** status in the growing empire. Many of these and others converted to Islam.

Today, Muslims expect to spread Islam, not by military conquest, but by example to those who feel inside that this is the right path for them. There have been many converts to Islam in the West, including Britain.

Jihad is also about the problems of conquering the self. It is difficult for many people, particularly in the western world, to adapt Muslim religious practice into the obligations of modern life. For instance, think about fitting **salah** (prayer) into a non-Muslim working environment at school or at work.

Yet jihad is not only about adjusting Muslim ritual to western culture. It is also about trying to make yourself a better Muslim. Quite often, this means a battle between what a person **would like** to do and what the rules of Islam say that a person **ought to** do; a battle perhaps between being selfish and being aware of other people's needs.

THINGS TO DO

1 As a class think of situations where there may be a conflict between what an individual might want to do for selfish reasons, and what that person ought to. Think also of a situation in which an individual's rights need to be defended.

2 What is the difference between inner and outer jihad? Describe in writing what you understand about it using a real or imagined situation.

3 Do you think that it is easier or more difficult to be a Muslim in a country where the main religion is Islam? How do you think this compares with being a Muslim in Britain? Discuss first in pairs, or groups of 3/4, then share with the rest of the class.

The Qur'an says this about Jihad:

Those who believe, and suffer
Exile and strive with might
And main, in God's cause,
With their goods and their persons,
Have the highest rank
In the sight of God:
They are the people
Who will achieve (salvation).
(*Sura 9 5:20*)

It is usually taken to mean that Holy War is not the only interpretation of Jihad. Even from the early period of the Muslim Empire, Jihad has also meant the struggle to develop a true faith in God and not to be led astray by the temptations of earthly power and material wealth in this world.

Some temptations are not as obvious as one might think. The following is adapted from a story told to Muslim children.

Long ago, when the Blessed Prophet Muhammad was alive, there also lived a man called Abu Talha. Now Abu Talha possessed a beautiful garden and spent many a happy hour in it. He felt that Allah had blessed him with much good fortune and liked to perform the afternoon Prayer in his garden.

One afternoon as usual, Abu Talha prepared to pray but his concentration was broken by the sound of the sweetest birdsong. He looked up and perched on a date palm was the most beautiful bird Abu Talha had ever seen. It had emerald green wings and a brilliant red tail. Its head was the yellow of burnished gold while from its jet black beak flowed the most beautiful music.

Abu Talha completely forgot about what he had intended to do. He could not help but stare at the beauty of this extraordinary bird. Finally, the bird finished its song and flew away and Abu Talha remembered why he was there. He felt ashamed and continued with his Prayer.

The following afternoon, Abu Talha was praying as usual. In the middle of his Prayer, he was interrupted by the singing of the beautiful bird

which had returned. This time the bird prepared to build a nest. Abu Talha found that it was impossible to continue with his devotions. He could not remember how far he had got to, and in great distress gave up.

He decided to visit the Prophet Muhammad (pbuh) and explained his problem.

'I have a beautiful garden with flowers, trees full of fruit and an exquisite bird whose song breaks one's heart. I cannot pray there any longer, O Prophet, because these beauties distract me from Prayer and my obligations to Allah. Please accept the gift of my garden to the Muslims of Madina to enjoy in their hours of leisure.'

The Prophet Muhammad was happy to receive the gift of Abu Talha's garden, and Abu Talha once again could perform his Prayers without further disruptions.

The moral here is that it is important to not even let the beauty of nature get in the way of your duties to God because God comes first.

THINGS TO DO

1 Think of another situation in which a duty/duties to God could easily be interfered with. How would you correct it?

2 Make a painting or drawing of Abu Talha's garden. It could be designed as a mural or montage, either a single or joint effort.

3 One Arabic word to describe a religious scholar is **mujtahid**, literally 'one who strives/works hard'. Why do you think that is?

4 Compare the two main types of Jihad. In what ways are they similar; in what ways different? Explain your answer.

Life After Death

Saliha was alone for the first time since she arrived in Pakistan with her parents and elder brother four days ago. Four days ago . . . it seemed as though an age had passed since then. She held in her hand a photograph of Grandfather. Such a gentle man. She remembered visiting her mother's parents for the first time as a very small girl. He had smiled at her . . . such a wonderful smile and taken her to a local cafe where he had bought her the most delicious lemonade in the world.

Last year, her grandparents had visited them in England and stayed for several months. Grandfather was already very frail. They all seemed to sense that they might not have him around for much longer. Now he was gone. Aunty had telephoned them a week ago to warn them that the end was near. At least they had four days to get used to him going. He had died early this morning. Now he was buried.

His body had been taken to the mosque and prepared for burial. The women had bade him farewell before that. Her grandmother was very brave. She had held Saliha's hand, eyes glistening with tears but not crying, a hint of a smile on her face. Turning to Saliha, she whispered, 'He is returning to God, the home of all good souls.'

Saliha did not really understand what she meant but it seemed as though grandmother was sad but not distraught. Her grief was not bitter.

Later, Saliha asked her mother what grandmother had meant. Her mother looked at her and smiled. 'Back home in England we do not always live with Muslim belief and custom on an everyday basis as our relatives do here. Your grandmother was talking about what is happening to your grandfather now that he has ended his earthly life. As a good man, your grandfather's soul is waiting for the Day of Judgement in **barzakh**, which is a kind of empty place, a limbo. At the Day of Judgement or sometimes we say **akhira**, your grandmother thinks that because he was a good Muslim, God will send your grandfather to Heaven, to **janna**, his natural home.'

'What's janna like?' asked Saliha.

'Hmm. That's not easy to answer because no one can be sure. Only the Prophet (pbuh) ever visited it. But we think that there are seven heavens in janna, and the more virtuous you are, you get to stay in the heaven nearest God, Who is in the seventh heaven. Ordinary people have to have their bodies purified and anointed and then wrapped in white sheets, just like grandfather – three for a man and five for a woman. One of grandfather's sheets was extra special because he had dipped it in the waters of Zam Zam when he went on Hajj as a young man. Do you know that people who die for the faith have already in a sense been purified and they are buried where they died without any preliminary preparations? They have a very special place in heaven, too.'

Now Saliha was alone, she was trying to absorb it all. It had been the first death in her family during her short life. It had been strange and unsettling at first. She had felt ignorant. Talking to her mother helped. She felt sad but perhaps grandmother was right. In which case, she should feel happy for her grandfather.

THINGS TO DO

1 As a class discuss why Muslim children in Britain might be ignorant of some Muslim customs which are taken for granted in countries where Islam is the dominant religion. Take care to remember that this may not generally be the case.

2 Why do you think that talking to her mother had helped Saliha to cope better with her grandfather's death?

3 Have you ever lost someone/something dear to you? Write about it or draw a real or imagined situation which is based on this idea.

4

CARE OF THE EARTH

Creation

Say: 'God is the Creator
Of all things: He is
The One, the Supreme and
Irresistible.'
(*Sura* 13:16)

In Muslim belief, God (Allah), created everything. He created the heavens and the earth and all the angels, including one named **Iblis**. God made **Adam**, the first human being, out of clay and taught him the names of all things. God told the angels to bow before Adam. They all obeyed save Iblis, who was proud. He said, 'I am made of fire and he is of clay. I am better than he,' said Iblis and refused to bow before Adam.

God became angry at his disobedience and banished Iblis from Paradise until the Day of Judgement. Iblis was shocked at the harshness of his punishment and vowed to avenge himself on Adam.

Adam wanted for nothing in God's garden in Paradise. He wanted neither food nor drink. Everything was provided for him. God saw that Adam needed more than the trees and rivers for company.

One night while he was asleep, God took part of Adam's left rib and created woman for his companion. Her name was **Hawwa'** (Eve). Adam was overjoyed now that he could share God's Paradise with her and talk to her.

God told Adam that he could live in Paradise with Hawwa' and they could eat and drink as much as they wanted in the garden except for the fruit of a particular tree. If they disobeyed Him, they would be punished. God also warned them that they had a powerful enemy in Iblis and to be wary of him. But Iblis (also known as Satan and the embodiment of evil), tempted Adam and Hawwa' out of Paradise.

Then began Satan to whisper
Suggestions to them ...
He said: 'Your Lord
Only forbade you this tree,
Lest ye should become angels
Or such beings as live for ever.'
So by deceit he brought about
Their fall.
(*Sura* 7:20, 22)

Once Adam and Hawwa' had eaten the fruit, they became aware of their nakedness and sewed leaves together to cover themselves.

When God saw them, He knew at once that they had disobeyed Him and He cast them out of Paradise to live and die on earth. Adam begged God's forgiveness, Who in His great mercy not only forgave him but made an agreement or covenant with him. Adam and his descendants were to be stewards of the earth.

Just as Muhammad was the last of the prophets, Adam was the first, and one tradition tells that God gave him the Black Stone which Adam later built into the wall of the Ka'aba (see page 28).

THINGS TO DO

1 How do you think the beginnings of creation happened? Present your ideas visually and/or in words.

2 Why do you think that God wanted the angels to bow down before Adam?

3 Write about a real or imaginary situation in which you were persuaded to do something that you knew you were not supposed to do. Say why you did it, and how you felt afterwards.

The Environment . . . Khalifa

To be Muslim is to be green, not only in the religious sense but also in the environmental sense. It is a tradition that the Prophet Muhammad himself (pbuh) is identified by the colour green as is Islam. Many Muslim states have green flags.

> It is He Who hath made
> You (His) agents, inheritors
> Of the earth
> (Sura 6:165)

The word for 'agents' is **khala'ifa**, in the plural in Arabic. **Khalifa** in the singular is used to describe the idea that everyone has responsibility for caring about God's world and to maintain order and the natural balance. We are all God's agents, khala'ifa.

Anything which upsets the natural balance goes against God's wishes.

The destruction of the rain forest.

The explosion at the Chernobyl nuclear power plant in the Ukraine, which contaminated the atmosphere and increased the rate of cancer in the surrounding population.

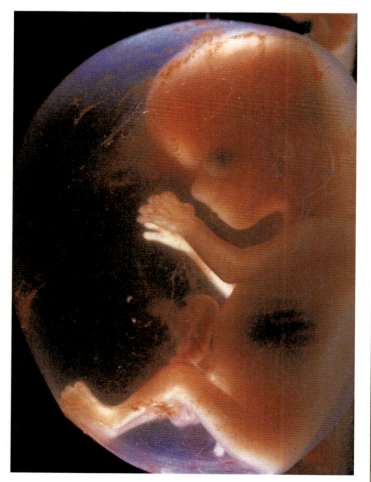

THINGS TO DO

1 Look at the two pictures above. Each represents a different threat to the natural balance. Explain how each relates to khalifa and why.

2 What other environmental issues can you think of? How do they link up with *Sura 6:165*?

3 In groups, create together a picture which includes drawing/montage and words which express the idea of khalifa.

4 Write a short story where a person makes something special. Someone else damages it. How does the person who made it feel?

Animal Rights

One day, during the summer holidays, there was a knock at Peter's door. Peter opened it to find a thoroughly disgruntled Murad standing on the doorstep.

PETER What's the matter with *you*?

MURAD Sisters. I *hate* them, especially mine.

PETER O.K. Come in. I've got some Bon Jovi on tape upstairs. It might improve your mood.

Later on …

PETER You're not really listening, are you?

MURAD Sorry – but Layla is really getting on my nerves. She's into animal rights in a big way. Has RSPCA posters on the walls of her bedroom and a sticker in the car. She goes to meetings and conferences at weekends, organises money raising projects at lunchtime at school. You know the sort of thing – you've seen her – selling cakes and so on to other pupils.

PETER So, what's wrong with that?

MURAD Nothing – except now she wants us all to turn vegetarian like her and goes on about us not wearing fur and leather shoes. She talks about nothing else at home and is driving everyone mad because she's always going on about it. Look, I like animals like most people but I don't want them ruling my life like this. This morning was the last straw. It's my birthday treat the Saturday after next and I was going to ask you whether you'd come with me to the Laser Park. Dad would take us. But now Layla says that's the weekend she's agreed to go with her friend to an animal welfare convention and she wants Dad to take them. He can't take both of us to where we want to go. Anyway, she made such a fuss about it, I got fed up and came round here.

PETER Hmm. Yes, you've certainly got problems. Maybe Layla will calm down a bit as she gets older. My aunt was into animal rights and saving the environment when she was younger. She told us about the sit-ins and demonstrations she was involved in. Then she got her job and couldn't find time for all of it. She's still a strong supporter but I don't think she went on about it like your sister.

MURAD Yeah. Anyway, I hope you're right Layla's impossible at the moment.

PETER Is Islam really strict about animal rights? Is that why Layla feels so involved?

MURAD Islam teaches that we must care for God's creatures because He is the Creator of all. We all have a responsibility to animals as well as the environment. Sometimes we call this **khalifa**. No, Layla is just over the top about it, she and some of her friends.

How was Murad's problem sorted out?

The outcome was that Murad's father insisted that the birthday treat was a higher priority than Layla's wish to attend her convention. Therefore, two weeks later, the two boys went on Murad's birthday treat and Layla and her friend used the bus.

THINGS TO DO

1 Which do you think is the more important issue: Murad's birthday treat or Layla's animal rights convention? Explain your reasons.

2 Animal welfare is important in Islam because animals are part of God's creation. How far animal rights are taken is very much up to the individual. Do you agree or disagree with this point of view?

5

THE WORD

Waiting for . . . The Word

This picture shows a mountain cave in a hot, rocky, harsh terrain. Imagine what it must be like to sit in the cave and look out on a desert wilderness.

In this cave fourteen hundred years ago, a man was to be found praying and meditating on what belief in God really meant. His name was Muhammad. He was a pious man, a member of an important tribe in Arabia at that time, called **Quraysh**, who had long been settled in a place called Makkah. Muhammad's particular family had responsibility for the care of the keys of the ancient sanctuary of Makkah, the Ka'aba, a great honour. At that time, Quraysh worshipped many gods and they had erected idols to them in the Ka'aba. Among the gods worshipped was the chief god, called Allah.

Muhammad had been brought up within this background. He knew that the Ka'aba was a holy shrine and that in one corner, it contained a black stone. No one knew for certain why the black stone was there. The people of Makkah knew only that the black stone was special and had been given to them in the days of the long distant past, perhaps as long ago as the time when Makkah was founded.

But this was the time of ignorance (**jahiliyya**), and the people of Makkah had forgotten many things about their past and about their Ka'aba.

Muhammad was different. He knew instinctively that there was more to the existence of the Ka'aba than a mere temple for many gods and goddesses. He searched within himself for the truth. He spent days on Mount Hira, in solitude and contemplation. He prayed. At home in Makkah, he performed the ancient rite of **tawaf**, which is the walking round the Ka'aba, seven times. He observed the festivals and the fairs attached to the Ka'aba. People from all over Arabia visited Makkah and its sanctuary, and because of this Makkah grew rich.

Yet something was wrong. Muhammad sensed it. A few other pious Qurayshis sensed it too. These people were referred to as **hanifs** (taken to mean searchers after religious truth). Some travelled long distances in their quest for the truth. One man travelled the long dusty road to Bosra in Syria, only to be told by a holy man there that a great prophet was about to appear among the people he had just left. So he returned home to Makkah to wait.

Read!

Every year during the month of Ramadan special rituals were observed by the people of Makkah. Muhammad would go to Mount Hira and pray on his own at this time. He gave food to the poor who came to him.

One night, the Angel Gabriel brought him the command of God.

'He came to me,' said the Apostle of God, 'while I was asleep, with a coverlet of brocade whereon was some writing and said "Read!"
I said, 'What shall I read?'
He pressed me with it so tightly that I thought it was death; then he let me go and said,
"Read!"
I said, "What shall I read?"
He pressed me with it again so that I thought it was death; then he let me go and said,
"Read!"
He pressed me with it the third time so that I thought it was death and said,
"Read!"
I said, "What then shall I read?" – and this I said only to deliver myself from him, lest he should do the same to me again.
He said:

> Read!
> In the name
> Of thy Lord and Cherisher,
> Who created –
>
> Created man, out of
> A (mere) clot
> Of congealed blood:
>
> Read! And thy Lord
> Is most Bountiful,
>
> He Who taught
> (The use of) the Pen,
>
> Taught man that
> Which he knew not.
> (*Sura* 96:1–5)

So I read it, and he departed from me. And I awoke from my sleep, and it was as though these words were written on my heart.

This account from traditional literature tells how Muhammad received the first revelation from God through the Angel Gabriel, in the fortieth year of his life (about 610 CE). For the remainder of his life (he died in 632 CE) Muhammad continued to receive revelations. Some time after his death the revelations were written down and collected into the book in which we have them today. Together, they are called the **Qur'an**, the sayings or proclamations of God.

The purpose of the revelations is to recall people to the true path of God. There is no God but God and Muhammad, praises and blessings be upon him, is his apostle (or messenger).

THINGS TO DO

1. In pairs. Turn to your neighbour and in TWO MINUTES say what your hopes and ambitions are, and why. Then it is your neighbour's turn. General discussion afterwards. Was it difficult?

2. Look at the picture. Imagine yourself in the cave, looking out over this scene. Write two paragraphs about what you feel and what your thoughts are.

3. Draw a picture of the perfect place, real or imagined, where you can go when you want to think something through without interruption.

4. Muhammad was different from most of the people among whom he lived. Explain why he was different.

5. In your own words describe how Muhammad was visited by the Angel Gabriel and what happened.

6. How do you think that Muhammad would have been able to tell his family and friends about his experience? Would it have been easy/difficult? Discuss first in groups and then as a class.

People of the Book

The old man, Bahira, was preoccupied with his prayers and did not notice the small caravan of travellers approaching out of the desert. Even if he had, he would not have considered it anything out of the ordinary. Many caravans of merchants, heading in all destinations to the rich cities of the Syrian coast, passed by his hermit's cell. He looked forward to conversations with itinerant visitors to relieve his solitude. Some of the regular ones he knew quite well.

The small caravan was quite close when at last the old monk looked up. 'Strangers,' he thought, 'tribesmen from the deserts far to the south.'

Then he noticed that the caravan of a dozen or so camels and some tribesmen were led by a man well past middle years and a young boy. Something about the boy arrested the old monk's attention. As they came closer, the Bahira stiffened. Many years of Christian meditation and prayer had given him an almost instinctive awareness of spiritual growth in others.

The caravan had stopped. The eyes in the lean and sunburnt face of its leader smiled at him. 'May we rest here for the night? We have been travelling many hours without meeting anyone. We will feed and water our camels, and ourselves. But conversation with someone from these parts is what we crave most.'

The Christian monk smiled and nodded his assent. After the caravan had settled itself for the night, the caravan's leader and the young boy sat with the old man and engaged him in conversation.

'I am a merchant from Makkah far to the south and I am travelling to Bosra to trade. My name is **Abu Talib** and this is my nephew **Muhammad ibn 'Abd Allah**.'

The hermit looked at the boy and said: 'You have a future designed for you by the One True God. You will be the prophet of your people.'

This is a fictionalised version of one of the Muslim traditions which foretell that even as a child, Muhammad, the Prophet of Islam, was seen to be a special person.

The hermit was not the only Christian to recognise Muhammad's future prophethood. After his terrifying first encounter with the Angel Gabriel, Muhammad sought reassurance from a Makkan Christian, **Waraqa ibn Naufal**, that the experience was truly from God and not from evil spirits or **jinn**.

THINGS TO DO

1 Why do you think that there are special stories foretelling Muhammad's prophethood? How do they help people to believe his message?

2 In pairs, discuss how it is possible to make judgements about strangers without knowing them. For instance, are they nice or awful? What is it about them and you which makes up your mind? Share your ideas with the class. Are first impressions always right?

Traditions such as these link Islam with the two other great monotheistic religions to come out of the Middle East, Judaism and Christianity. The Jews played a significant, if negative role, in the years Muhammad ruled Madina, where he went after the Hijra or Migration from Makkah. In Madina, the tradition relates that the Jews set out to help destroy the fledgling Muslim community. It was for this reason that Muhammad changed the direction of worship (**qiblah**) away from Jerusalem to Makkah and the Ka'aba.

However, it is also clear that the Jews are to be respected. The first codification (writing down) of God's laws, the Torah (**Tawrah**), was sent to the Prophet Moses (**Musa**) in Arabic, and so formed one of the bases of the Muslim concept of **Din** or True Religion of the One God.

After a period of time, God also sent Isa (Jesus) with the Gospels (**Injil**) so that people would be guided to the true path.

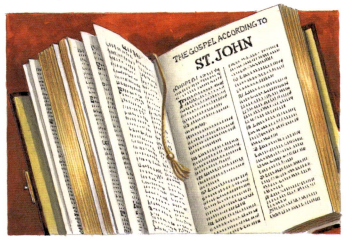

It is because God sent the Torah to the Jews and the Gospels to the Christians that in Islam they are referred to as **People of the Book**. Muslims also regard themselves as People of the Book because of the sending down of the revelations of the Holy Qur'an.

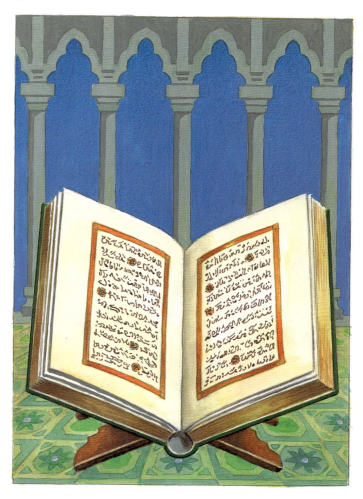

THINGS TO DO

1 Who are the People of the Book in Islam and why?

2 Why do you think tradition is important in Islam?

3 Many schools and families have traditions which are remembered at different times of the year. Does your school or family? If so, say what it/they is/are. If not, try and explain why such traditions exist.

The Word Revealed

Peter has arrived at Murad's house in the late afternoon, ushered up to his bedroom door by his mother. Peter pauses outside Murad's door because he can hear his friend's voice. Is he talking to himself? Murad is not exactly singing, neither is he speaking in an ordinary voice.

Peter knocks on the door. A cheery 'Come in' is the response, and Peter opens the door and enters.

MURAD Oh, Hi! Just a minute while I put this away.

With great care, the book is closed and Murad stands to put it on a shelf.

PETER Look, I'm sorry if I sound rude, but what exactly were you doing?

Peter's face shows great amazement.

MURAD (laughs) Only reading the Qur'an. That's how I was taught to read it by the **imam** (prayer leader) at the mosque. My mother likes me to do some every day.

Peter still does not look convinced.

MURAD Look, all Muslim children have to learn to read the Holy Qur'an. That's how we learn the word of God just as it was revealed to our Prophet Muhammad (pbuh) 1,400 years ago. The Holy Qur'an is the word of God.

PETER But why do you have to say it in ... **that** way?

MURAD (grinning): I know it must sound strange to you. We read it in that sing-song way partly because it helps us learn it, and partly because it is the word of God written in classical Arabic and not in the ordinary language of everyday speech. It is a holy language which needs a special way of saying it. Look, I'll show you.

Murad retrieves his Qur'an from the shelf. He sits down again, opens it and begins to sound the words, almost in song (**intones**), whilst gently rocking to and fro. This time, Peter realises that the words are not in English. Inwardly, he feels a great respect for his friend and the way Murad accepts the demands of his faith. Murad continues for about a minute and stops.

PETER Do you understand those words?

MURAD Most of them because my parents and the imam have explained what they mean. Classical Arabic is quite difficult to learn unless you are really clever. A special name is given to those who really know and understand the Qur'an. They are called **hafiz**. I don't think I am clever enough for that but I hope to know most of the Holy Book when I'm older.

PETER And you have to do that on top of your school work?

Murad nods and returns the Qur'an to its place on the shelf. The two boys settle down to do something else.

THINGS TO DO

1 Explain how the Qur'an is the Word of God for Muslims.

2 Why is the Qur'an recited in a special way?

3 Do you play a musical instrument or a particular sport or have the sort of interest which makes regular, time consuming demands on you? Do you sometimes wish you could just go and watch television or be with your friends, instead of having to spend time on your hobby or interest as well as your school work and other home obligations? Describe how you feel.

6

JOURNEYS

Life is like a journey. Muslims accept that God is there at the beginning:

God is part of growing up:

God is part of marriage:

God is part of parenthood:

God is part of old age:

And God is there at the end of life.

THINGS TO DO

1 Given above are just a few examples of how God is part of human life. Draw and describe in a paragraph for each, two other examples.

2 Draw or describe your own life journey as a chart, map or comic strip. Mark on special things and different stages in your life.

Hajj

Hajj is the main Muslim pilgrimage and involves a special journey to the birthplace of the Prophet Muhammad, Makkah, and its ancient place of worship, the Ka'aba. It is one of the main obligations of Muslim life. If it is at all possible, a Muslim must undertake at least one Hajj in his or her lifetime.

The practice of Hajj goes back to well before the rise of Islam. Muslim tradition links the pilgrimage with some of the rituals of the true religion of God (Din), which had been lost before the birth of Muhammad.

Together with other aspects of the true religion of God recovered by Muhammad, the Prophet also restored the Hajj. Ever since his death, Muslims have continued to perform the special rituals of the pilgrimage ceremonies.

The Hajj is an obligation that all Muslims are committed to undertake if at all possible. That means that a person can only perform the Hajj if he or she can afford to go, and that the pilgrim's family and home are well looked after while they are away. It is said that a Muslim who cannot afford to go on Hajj, attends in spirit during the Hajj festival. Those people who can afford to go, undertake to remember those who are not able to go.

Like all the obligations of Islam the Hajj makes everyone equal. Everyone wears special clothes and forsakes worldly dress and vanity; and sexual activity is forbidden during this time. Pilgrims are said to be in a state of **ihram**, or of ritual purity.

Hajj is a time when people think hard about the purpose of their lives and about God. It is one of the times when Muslims are not concerned about their everyday lives because they have temporarily left that behind them. They are free to concentrate fully on what God means to them.

The Hajj is a deeply spiritual experience and pilgrims have to be old enough to understand what they are doing. Children do sometimes accompany their parents but often are too young to be fully fledged

Pilgrims dressed for the Hajj.

Hajjis (people who have been on the Hajj). They are not yet mature enough to understand the significance of the ceremonies and prayers.

THINGS TO DO

1 Why is the Hajj an important part of Muslim practice?

2 What are the pilgrims expected to do before leaving Hajj?

3 The Hajj is 'a deeply spiritual experience'. What do you think that means?

A Journey of Self-discovery – The Hajj

Look at the picture above. It shows the Ka'aba and Haram Mosque at night. Around it is a whirlpool. But this whirlpool is not water; it is human. Hundreds and hundreds of people swirling round the Ka'aba. Looking at the picture makes you dizzy. The picture forces you to ask questions. Why should this be? Why are so many people gathered together at one time?

These people are participating in **tawaf**. It is a ritual which has been practised for centuries, as far back as the time of the Prophet Muhammad himself. A believer must walk round the Ka'aba seven times in an anti-clockwise direction, reciting special prayers. Tawaf may be practised at any time of the year, but it becomes especially significant at the time of the Hajj.

The Hajj is one of the main obligations placed on Muslims; it is one of the five pillars. However, it is different from the others in that the Hajj may be undertaken rarely or in certain circumstances not at all. The rules stipulate that all prospective pilgrims, or **Hajjis**, must be in good health and have ensured that all is in good order before they leave home. This means that he or she has adequately provided for those left at home, settled any personal disputes and met all debts. It may be difficult for some people to satisfy all these essentials.

Look once again at the picture on page 35. What is it like to be part of that swirling mass? The following was written by a Muslim and experienced Hajji, Abdul Hakim Murad, offering advice to the boxer, Mike Tyson, a convert to Islam when he was about to undertake his first Hajj.

> The Hajj is about returning to the centre, focusing on unity, letting the centripetal force of God win out for a few days over the dissipating trends of the world. Caught up in its rites, milling with the millions around the Holy Ka'aba like moths around a candle, we forget the four points of the compass and discover a liberating ability to connect with what lies beyond.
>
> ... I found my first Hajj so unfamiliar and astonishing that I prayed hardly at all. Nowhere else, not even at Disney World, do so many people come together in one place. Standing, praying, eating, talking with 2 million other men and women from every race is a dazzling confirmation of one's own insignificance and of the global fellowship that is Islam.
> (*The Independent*, 19 April 1995)

The fact that you are a single individual among perhaps as many as two million other pilgrims releases you from self-consciousness. Here, you are separated from your usual, everyday existence, your private cares as well as your public ones. Every day for almost two weeks, you participate in ceremonies with hundreds and thousands of other people.

Your mind allows itself to explore the meaning of your faith, your relationship with God. You become conscious that you have a relationship with all of these people, only a few of whom you will ever meet. There is a sense of fellowship in the faith shared with these strangers. Why is this? Your mind can only dimly begin to grasp the answer. You are too small, too incapable of understanding what is happening to you. You only know that you are participating in an ancient mystery which brings you and all your fellow pilgrims to a closer awareness of God. In a sea of

humanity, you are alone before your God. This is what Abdal Hakim Murad means about being liberated.

Mike Tyson, champion boxer and convert to Islam.

THINGS TO DO

1 How would you explain the Hajj to a non-Muslim? Is it possible to compare it with something else? Explain your answer.

2 The Hajj is an obligation which Muslims must undertake if at all possible, at least once in their lives. How do you think they might feel if they are unable to do so?

3 With the aid of a dictionary, what do you think is meant by 'the centripetal force of God?' Why do you think that Abdul Hakim Murad 'found [his] first Hajj so unfamiliar and astonishing'?

The Mosque

> And for me the earth has been made a mosque and a means of purification; therefore, if prayer overtakes any person of my community, he should say his prayers (wherever he is).
> (*Hadith*)

This **hadith**, or saying, of the Prophet Muhammad describes the whole earth as a place of prayer, a **mosque**. Private or formal prayers may be said anywhere a person happens to be.

However, it is also important for Muslims to gather together as a community or **ummah** (see pages 10–11) as part of worship. Since the time of the Prophet, people have congregated in buildings specially designed for prayer, or in private houses. The first mosques in Britain tended to be converted private houses because of the expense and difficulty in building purpose built ones.

A Muslim will only bow or prostrate him- or herself before God as part of prayer. The Arabic word for a mosque is **masjid**, the place of prostration.

Many mosques are beautifully designed buildings but they have also to be both practical and functional, and these aspects are reflected in the design.

The most prominent feature of a purpose built mosque, is a slim tower or **minaret**. The call to prayer or **adhan**, is intended to come from here but in Britain the number of times this happens is restricted to once or twice a year. The authorities say that they have a duty to protect local non-Muslim residents from noise at unsocial hours.

On entering the mosque, worshippers must remove shoes as a sign of respect. They have to prepare themselves for worship by ritual washing, or **wudu**, and there must be separate facilities for men and women. There may be separate entrances to the prayer hall for men and women, particularly in the bigger mosques where there is often an upstairs area for women overlooking the hall itself.

The prayer hall is usually quite plain except for framed quotations from the Holy Qur'an hanging on the walls. Nothing that could be interpreted as idol worship is permitted. The prayer hall will be the largest area of the building and some mosques will accommodate an occasional larger gathering in a courtyard connecting with the prayer hall.

Prayers are said facing in the direction of Makkah (the **qiblah**) and a niche or **mihrab** will be set in the qiblah wall for the guidance of the congregation.

There will be a **minbar**, or pulpit for the sermon, and this is almost invariably placed on the qiblah wall to one side, usually the right.

Finally, there is usually a room for the dead. When a person dies, their body has to be specially prepared for burial.

Traditionally, the mosque is built centrally within a Muslim community because it has to be accessible at prayer times. Therefore, people live and work within easy reach of their local mosque. Obviously, this pattern of living is more suited to an urban rather than a rural lifestyle. The world of classical Islam is distinguished by the development of an urban culture rather than one based in the countryside. Even today, most British Muslims are town dwellers.

THINGS TO DO

1 The Arabic word for a mosque is **masjid**, the place of prostration. Why do you think that is?

2 Why does the **mosque** have a special place in Muslim communities?

3 Describe briefly what the following words mean:
hadith   minaret   qiblah
mosque   adhan   mihrab
ummah   wudu   minbar.

4 In groups, or as a class, discuss whether or not the use of the **minaret** should be restricted. Explain your reasons.

Prayer – Coming Closer to God

And establish regular prayers
At the two ends of the day
And at the approaches of the night:
For those things which are good
Remove those that are evil:
Be that the word of remembrance
To those who remember (their Lord).
(*Sura 11:114*)

From the beginning of Islam, prayer, **salah**, has formed an integral part of everyday life. Salah is the second pillar of Islam and the most important act of worship, **ibadah**.

Salah is different from private prayer, **du'a**, although both forms are practised. Whilst private prayer can take place at any time, salah is the term used for the formal act of worship which occurs at set times of the day. People may practice salah at home or wherever they happen to be; but it is expected that on important days, such as Fridays and festivals, salah will be observed in the mosque. As with many other aspects of Islam, communal salah reinforces awareness of the community of Muslims, the ummah.

The Friday prayers, or **jum'ah** prayers, have always been important. It is the occasion when a sermon, or **khutbah**, is often preached from the **minbar**, or pulpit, particularly in countries where Islam is the main religion.

A minbar

There is no division in Islam between politics and religion so the message preached can often be political as well as religious. The Prophet Muhammad was both a religious and political leader.

In the days of huge Muslim empires, such as the Abbasid, Ottoman, and Mughal Empires, the name of the ruler was declared during the khutbah. During Friday prayers worshippers were reminded of who exactly was in charge of the empire or kingdom and to whom earthly loyalty was due.

During the first years following the 1979 Islamic Revolution in Iran, the khutbahs of Ayatollah Khomeini, who became the best known of all Iranian leaders, attracted a lot of press attention in the west. The Ayatollah was a deeply respected religious leader in Iran as well as being the political leader of the revolution.

THINGS TO DO

1 Prayer times are part of a centuries-old tradition which allows people to live and work near a mosque and attend prayers regularly. How do you think this affects devout Muslims living in Britain who often live a long way from where they work or who work for a non-Muslim employer? A class discussion; or in groups first and then shared with the whole class.

2 Why is **salah** important? Imagine that you are explaining this to a non-Muslim.

3 There is no division between politics and religion in Islam. Why is this and how might it influence different aspects of Muslim life?

Prayer – How We Do It

There are five acts of prayer scheduled each day. According to Muslim tradition, when Muhammad visited the seven heavens during his **mi'raj**, or night journey, God commanded that Muslims should pray 5,000 times a day. Muhammad pleaded that human beings were too weak to comply with such a difficult task. Eventually the command was reduced to five salah a day.

Each prayer has a special name, and the mosque will list the times of each on a notice board. The times vary in Britain because of the difference between daylight hours in winter and summer.

- **Fajr** – between the first light of day and sunrise.
- **Zuhr** – after the sun has moved away from the centre of the sky.
- **Asr** – between mid-afternoon and sunset.
- **Maghrib** – after sunset and before the final light of day.
- **Isha** – after nightfall and before dawn.

Formal prayer involves the whole person. First of all, there is the formalised washing or wudu before prayer. Men are separated from women. The head, mouth, nose, arms, feet and ankles must be washed three times, and the ears and neck thoroughly cleansed. Then there are the prayers and movements followed by all Muslims. When they are old enough, children learn how to pray in this way.

The **mu'addhin** (or **muezzin**), calls people to pray at the stipulated times. In Muslim countries, this is when the call to prayer is broadcast from the minarets of the mosques. In Britain, Muslims are not permitted to do this on a regular basis, although some mosques are permitted to call publicly once or twice a year. The call is usually repeated in the mosque.

Wherever they happen to be in the world, all Muslims face towards the direction of the Ka'aba in Makkah when they pray, which is usually called the **qiblah**. The qiblah for British Muslims is towards the south west.

It is customary for women to pray separately from men. This safeguards their modesty and dignity. Often a mosque will have a special area where women will assemble.

To pray in Islam is to prostrate yourself before God; to fall down before the Creator. A Muslim does not bow to a human being; only to God.

The movements of the prayer ritual have names. Completion of one set of movements is called a **rak'ah**. There are a varying number of rak'ahs for each scheduled set of prayers: Fajr – two; Maghrib – three; Zuhr, Asr and Isha – four.

Takbir | Right hand over left | Ruku | Qiyam

Sujud | Kneeling again with palms on knees / Sujud again | salam

THINGS TO DO

1 On a sheet of paper draw the prayer positions, explaining what each one is.

2 Prayer is intended to lead the believer closer to God. In a piece of written work or a drawing express how the ritual of salah helps this process.

3 A Muslim bows to no human being. In pairs, think of at least 3 situations where this rule might cause problems. Then share with the rest of the class.

7

COMMUNITY

A Western Religion

Fozia Bora, Jamil Ali and Sada Irfan work for Q-News, a weekly newspaper for young British Muslims.

Islam originated in the Middle East and then spread worldwide, as you can see from the map on p 9.

Islam arrived in the West later than Judaism and Christianity. Most Muslim communities have grown up since the end of the Second World War. Islam is now officially the second largest religion after Christianity in Britain. Many immigrant Muslim families go back more than two generations. Their children were born and educated here often to university level. British culture is part of their background as well as their Islamic heritage.

The English language has helped to bring different Muslim groups together. Many Muslims communicate more easily in English even though their families originated from different parts of the world, speaking the languages of Pakistan, Africa and the Middle East. All Muslim children brought up in Britain speak English because they attend school here.

As a result, a British form of Islamic culture appears to be evolving. Young, educated British Muslims

show an increasing awareness and interest in the more scholarly and religious literature of Islam. More so than their parents, perhaps, who came from backgrounds offering fewer opportunities. It will be interesting to see how British Islam continues to develop in the future.

THINGS TO DO

1 Many Muslim children speak two languages fluently: the language from where their parents came; and English. Firstly in groups, then as a class, think about the advantages and problems this could bring to the children and their parents.

2 What choices are there for British Muslim children? Are they any different for non-Muslim children? Think about education, job ambitions, what to do in leisure time.

Sharing . . . Zakat

But it is righteousness . . .
. . . To spend of your substance,
Out of love for Him,
For your Kin,
For orphans,
For the needy,
For the wayfarer,
For those who ask,
And for the ransom of slaves . . .
. . . And practice regular charity.
(*Sura* 2:177)

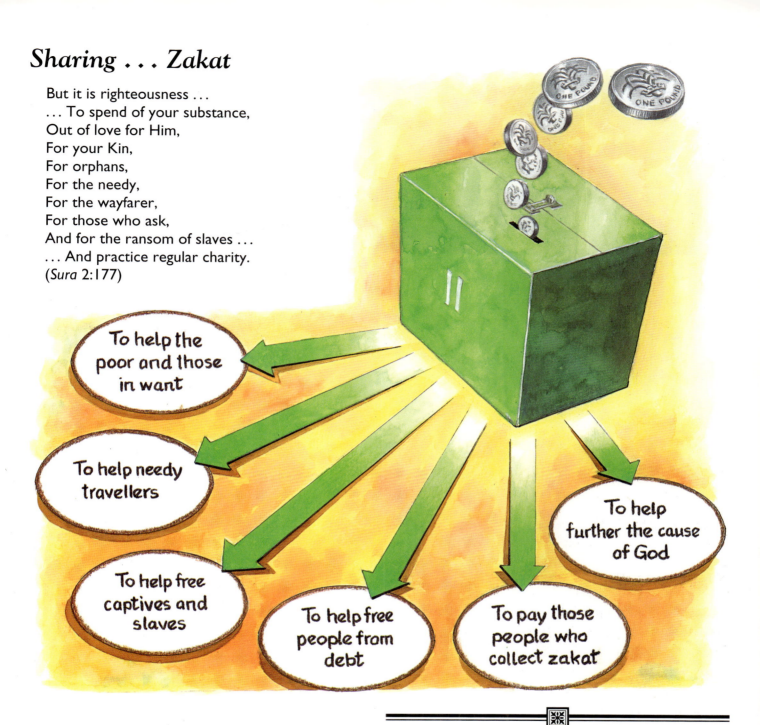

To help the poor and those in want

To help needy travellers

To help free captives and slaves

To help free people from debt

To pay those people who collect zakat

To help further the cause of God

Murad is given £2 per week pocket money and adds to it by doing odd jobs for his parents, such as washing and polishing the car. Occasionally, he earns extra money babysitting for his neighbours.

Every week when he visits the mosque, Murad will donate 5p, perhaps more if he has earned more, to **zakat**. All Muslims have an obligation as one of the Five Pillars of Islam to allocate 2½% of their earnings to zakat and in every mosque stands a zakat box.

The money is collected and is used in different ways.

THINGS TO DO

1 Make a list of the different kinds of purposes zakat is aimed at.

2 Do you receive pocket money or have you a means of earning some money out of school? When you receive your money, is any of it already committed to being spent on a necessity, for instance? How do you feel about this?

Muslims Together – Ramadan

Look at the picture. The sun is rising above the horizon. During the month of **Ramadan**, Muslims must eat and drink nothing from the moment the sun rises to the moment it sets. When Ramadan falls during British midsummer, it makes the hours of fasting very long indeed.

Peter finds Murad sitting by himself during break. His friend is not as bright as usual.

PETER What's the matter? I thought you'd want to practice at the basketball courts.

MURAD It's nothing. I'm feeling a bit low because it's the second day of the fast.

PETER What fast?

MURAD Ramadan. It's what Muslims have to do every year.

PETER What! Even you?

MURAD Yes. I'm old enough and, anyway, I want to do it. My whole family is fasting except for my little sister. She's too young.

PETER So, who's expected to do it?

MURAD All Muslims. **Sawm**, or fasting in English, is one of the obligations of our faith. Every year during the Muslim month of Ramadan, we have to fast. Only those who are too ill, too young or women who are pregnant are excused. People travelling do not fast but are expected to make up for it later on.

PETER That's tough. So you can't eat. But surely you can drink can't you?

MURAD No. Not during the whole day. We can't eat or drink from the time the sun comes up to when it sets. We do eat and drink before sunrise and after sunset. We get up very early and have something which will keep us going all day. Mind you, it's a bit hard in the summer.

PETER But you must feel hungry when you see the rest of us eating?

MURAD Yes, but I'm getting used to it. It's important that we fast at this time. All Muslims everywhere in the world fast during Ramadan. It's one of the things we do together. I think that's what keeps us going. We support each other. Then at the end of it we have a big party. It's a bit like your Christmas. For three days we eat and drink and give presents and visit each other. Our holy book, the Qur'an says that it was during the month of Ramadan that the Qur'an was given to us by God. So it's a very special time.

PETER Amazing. I realise it's important for you. But … well, I'll try not to eat my lunch in front of you.

MURAD (grins) Thanks. Your understanding helps.

THINGS TO DO

1 In your own words, explain why there is an annual fast during Ramadan.

2 Fasting is common to many world religions. Why do you think this is?

3 What would you give up for a month for a good cause? Why?

Saving Up for the Cause of God

Have you ever wanted to do something or buy something important so badly that you saved up all your pocket money over a long time and earned extra money by doing odd jobs for people, like babysitting, or washing your parents' car, or perhaps cutting the grass?

Was it too much effort and you gave up in the end? Or were you so determined that you eventually succeeded? How long did it take you?

This is the Jamia Ghausia Mosque in Aylesbury, a town in Buckinghamshire. It took the Muslim community of Aylesbury 18 years to save up enough money, supplemented by a loan from a bank, to build their own mosque. They were determined to have a special building designed for Muslim worship to replace the converted house they had been using. The number of Muslims living in and around the town was also growing to an estimated 500 families at present.

Individuals were asked to contribute £1 each per week to this special cause. It took a long time. A site for the mosque had to be found and planning permission applied for from the local authority; an architect appointed to design the building, and a firm of builders to erect it.

Eventually, about £800,000 was raised, which was enough to build the mosque.

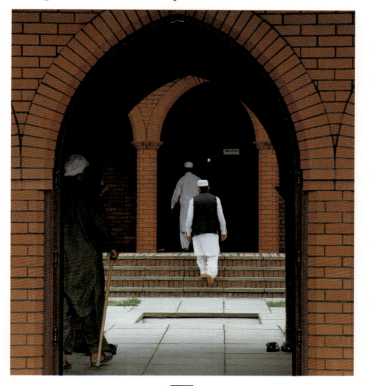

THINGS TO DO

1 Think about something important, real or imagined, that you would like to have but cannot afford. Write about how you would save up for it, with pictures to illustrate your account.

2 In a series of drawings, tell the story of how the Aylesbury mosque came to be built. Think about what else you could usefully add, for example, painting the walls.

3 Why do you think that the converted house became inadequate for the needs of the Muslim community? For class discussion, then to be written up in exercise books.

The fundraising is not finished yet because there are other essential items needed, such as books for the mosque library.

A number of people who worship at the mosque also have to go to local schools or out to work. Many work for non-Muslim employers, some of whom allow their Muslim employees to worship at the scheduled times, but not all. Either way, it means that the Muslim community does not meet as often as it might in a country where Islam is the main religion.

Meeting friends after Jum'ah Prayers at Aylesbury's mosque.

Their Imam, Abd-al Dayan Khizri, says that it is important for him to meet as many of the community as possible, just so that he can ensure that people are all right and he can care for their spiritual welfare. The numbers are too large for him to rely solely on the telephone for contact, but not as large as might be expected in a bigger town or city.

Therefore, the next major project for Aylesbury's Muslims is to build a community centre attached to the mosque, so that people can meet and socialise, perhaps at weekends when many Muslims will not be working.

The money for these projects is special and regarded as **sadaqah**, or raised for the cause of God. Collected through voluntary, selfless donations, the money is thought of as cleansed and, therefore, appropriate for such a purpose.

Market day in the centre of Aylesbury.

Money given to an emergency relief appeal, or to some other charity which helps less fortunate people, is also **sadaqah**. The money is donated out of concern and caring for others and not for the benefit of the giver.

THINGS TO DO

1 **Sadaqah** is for something special. In small groups of two or three, discuss why this is. Then as a class decide how you could apply sadaqah to a school project.

2 Describe at least three different uses, to which the proposed community centre might be put.

3 Why do you think the imam prefers working for a Muslim community the size of Aylesbury's, which is in a medium sized town, and not for one in an area the size of Sheffield or Bradford? Discuss as a class.

8

DIFFERENCES

Teenagers

Murad is listening to his favourite band on his head-phones. His parents will not let him play his CDs without them. Two of his friends, Peter and Jamal are playing a computer game on Murad's TV. A typical teenager's messy bedroom.

PETER Oh, no, I've died. You've beaten me yet again.

JAMAL Yeah. See, talent wins again. I'm sorry but you'll have to agree that I'm the expert.

PETER But I don't know how you do it – your Mum won't let you have a computer game.

JAMAL It's sad, isn't it. But thanks to my friend Murad here, I can practice on his.

MURAD Eh, what's that? (Takes off 'phones) You talking about me?

JAMAL I was telling Peter how my Mum won't allow me a computer game. I know they're expensive, but that's not the reason. You see, my Mum comes from a village in Pakistan, where her family was very strict about what she did. They didn't like it at all when she married my Dad, who was born here and was used to western ways. My Mum has tried to adapt to the different customs and traditions we have here. But it hasn't been easy for her. When she goes home for a visit, and we all go with her, her parents are very concerned that we are not all being led astray.
I feel sorry for my Mum because she is trying to be a good daughter and so she tries to be strict with us. Sometimes I get fed up with some things, but then in my religion I have to remember to be respectful towards my parents because they know what is best for me.

MURAD Yeah. Muslim teaching is very clear about what children owe their parents. Is it the same for you? (to Peter)

PETER I think so, but it is not always as spelt out as it seems to be with you. Teenagers are more used to rebelling against their parents in this country. But your parents (to Murad) don't mind about your pop music and computer games, do they?

MURAD No. But that's because they both converted to Islam when they had grown up, and were already used to pop and other forms of western music. They don't have a problem with that or computer games. Here, either of you want a game?

JAMAL Peter can if I can use your 'phones.

THINGS TO DO

1 Orthodox Muslims expect to comply with their parents' wishes. Do you think that there might be difficulties for Muslims brought up in a western country compared to those brought up in a country where Islam is the main religion? Or do you think it might make very little difference? Discuss as a class.

2 Jamal's mother will not allow him to have computer games at home. How do you think she might feel about him playing computer games at Murad's house? Does Jamal understand his mother's predicament? Write your answer as fully as possible, from both points of view.

3 Imagine that it will soon be your birthday and you would like to celebrate it with your friends – boys and girls, Muslims and non-Muslims. In groups, or individually, devise a plan (or plans) for a birthday celebration which would suit most people and not offend anyone. Write down your plans or use a series of drawings or cartoons.

How Do We Get On With People?

In Britain, we often associate such a scene with going on holiday, relaxing, getting away from it all. Our weather is so changeable, that such a picture tends to conjure up in people the wish to escape to warmth and pleasure.

But pleasure these days can carry a certain amount of risk. Because of the greenhouse effect, fair skins have to be careful about burning in the sun. It carries the risk of cancer. And so the idyllic picture carries a hint of threat within it. The possibility that the sunbaked beach ideal has a negative side to it is also true in Islam.

Many countries, where the largest religious group is Muslim, are in the hotter parts of the world. Countries like Egypt, Pakistan, and Malaysia. To people living there the sun does not carry the same attractions as it does in Britain. They have to live with the heat from day to day, and in some of these areas the sun can be an enemy.

For instance, if the monsoon does not fall in Bangladesh, then the consequences can be catastrophic. Insufficient rain can lead to reduced rice production and starvation. Too much rain can lead to serious flooding.

Muslim law has been developed over the centuries since the death of the Prophet Muhammad, in predominantly hot countries. Arabia, Muhammad's homeland, is mostly desert. Muslim law encourages both sexes to be discreet and modest in their dealings with each other; so in many Muslim countries women must cover themselves up in public and men are expected to dress modestly.

In Muslim countries, there are different opinions on how well covered the human body should be. But many women in these countries, would find it difficult to dress in public the way most women in Britain take for granted. Here, the matter of how you dress is left very much to individual taste.

THINGS TO DO

1 In Britain, and to a large extent in the rest of Europe and the USA, it is generally accepted that women can bathe topless if they choose to do so. What do you think Muslim people in countries where westerners go on holiday, feel about the freedom allowed women to bathe topless? Do you think that topless bathing should be allowed there? Or do you think that local custom should be respected by holiday makers? Debate the issue of topless bathing in holiday resorts in Muslim countries. Either for general class discussion or for a more formalised debate with two groups with appropriate speakers representing opposite points of view.

2 Write a newspaper report on the issue of topless bathing in Muslim countries EITHER for OR against.

3 On A3 or larger paper, create a montage of painting/drawing of both the attractions and dangers of the sun. If possible make use of holiday brochure pictures for the montage.

From Confrontation Towards . . .

This picture is from a film about the black militant, Malcolm X. He became famous in the 1960s in particular because he fought for the rights of the blacks in the United States of America. He was active in a radical militant group called the Black Power Movement.

The film shows how terrible life was for black people in the US. Poor education and discrimination meant that many black people were forced into a life of crime and degradation. Black people were often segregated from whites. That meant that black people were often not permitted to go into some of the public places where white people went, for instance, into certain shops, restaurants, and public conveniences. In many places black school children were not allowed to attend schools in white areas.

Malcolm X grew up hating white people and the system which allowed whites to dominate blacks. After a period when he lived as a petty criminal, he was arrested, convicted and sent to prison. While there, he became influenced by a militant form of Islam to such an extent that he reformed his personal life and became a convert.

In the 1960s many black people converted to Islam as a protest against the unfairness of a society which was mostly Christian but neglected the plight of the poor, especially blacks. One of the most famous converts of the time was Muhammad Ali, who as Cassius Clay had become the heavyweight boxing champion of the world.

Malcolm also was such a convert. He made use of his religious experience to reform other blacks but continued to hate whites.

The 1960s were a time of confrontation between blacks and whites in the US. In 1968, the Democratic Convention in Detroit, which had met to select a candidate for the next American presidential election, was overshadowed by violent racial riots.

Such riots seemed commonplace and often Malcolm X's Black Muslims were associated with such disturbances. Their salute was the clenched fist held high. It was a frightening period in modern American history.

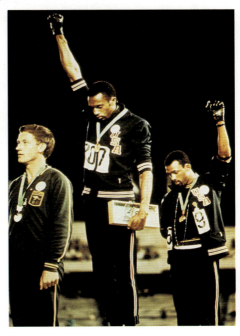

The 1968 Olympic Games in Mexico City. US medal winners Tommie Smith (gold) and John Carlos (bronze) give the Black Power salute at the award ceremony for the men's 200 metres.

THINGS TO DO

1 Why do you think there may have been race riots at the time of the US Democratic Convention in 1968?

2 What do you think is meant by 'he became influenced by a militant form of Islam'?

3 In groups or as a class discuss how deeply rooted tensions sometimes erupt in violence.

A New Understanding

Then Malcolm X's attitude to whites changed. As part of his obligation to his faith, he performed the Hajj and met many, many people from all over the world. Some were not only Muslim but white. He realised then that Islam was and is a universal religion. In Islam, the ummah, the Muslim community, is very important and *all* Muslims belong to it whatever their personal opinions, or ethnic origin.

The film shows how this new understanding alienated Malcolm from some of the members of his militant Islamic movement. They still favoured an aggressive attitude towards whites, not reconciliation. They thought Malcolm's new ideas threatened them and their movement so they murdered him.

This new attitude towards reconciliation is something that Nelson Mandela adopted in another country divided by racial apartheid, South Africa. Co-operation between blacks and whites is how Mandela sees the way forward for his country.

Nelson Mandela makes an appearance at the end of the film *Malcolm X*. He says that Malcolm's work and personal sacrifice contributed a great deal towards the idea of reconciliation between traditionally antagonistic ethnic groups. Malcolm had discovered that the whole world was his ummah.

THINGS TO DO

1 Why did the Hajj persuade Malcolm to change his mind about white people?

2 Have you ever completely changed your opinion about a person (or people) or about a problem or situation? Write an account of or a poem about your change of heart.

3 In the film, Malcolm X paid the price of his enlightened attitude with his death. Express in words or as a drawing the significance of his death.